Networks for Sustainability

Harnessing People Power to Deliver Your Goals

Sarah Holloway

www.sarahholloway.co.uk

sarah@sarahholloway.co.uk

First published in 2013 by Dō Sustainability

87 Lonsdale Road, Oxford OX2 7ET, UK

ISBN 978-1-909293-88-5 (eBook-ePub)

ISBN 978-1-909293-89-2 (eBook-PDF)

ISBN 978-1-909293-87-8 (Paperback)

A catalogue record for this title is available from the British Library.

Dō Sustainability strives for net positive social and environmental impact. See our sustainability policy at **www.dosustainability.com**.

Page design and typesetting by Alison Rayner

Cover by Becky Chilcott

For further information on Dō Sustainability, visit our website: **www.dosustainability.com**

DōShorts

Dō Sustainability is the publisher of DōShorts: short, high-value ebooks that distil sustainability best practice and business insights for busy, results-driven professionals. Each DōShort can be read in 90 minutes.

New and forthcoming DōShorts – stay up to date

We publish 3 to 5 new DōShorts each month. The best way to keep up to date? Sign up to our short, monthly newsletter. Go to **www.dosustainability.com/newsletter** to the Dō Newsletter. Some of our latest and forthcoming titles include:

- *How to Engage Youth to Drive Corporate Responsbility: Roles and Interventions* Nicolò Wojewoda
- *The Short Guide to Sustainable Investing* Cary Krosinsky
- *Strategic Sustainability: Why it Matters to Your Business and How to Make it Happen* Alexandra McKay
- *Sustainability Decoded: How to Unlock Profit Through the Value Chain* Laura Musikanski
- *Working Collaboratively: A Practical Guide to Achieving More* Penny Walker
- *Understanding G4: The Concise Guide to Next Generation Sustainability Reporting* Elaine Cohen
- *Leading Sustainable Innovation* Nick Coad & Paul Pritchard
- *Leadership for Sustainability and Change* Cynthia Scott & Tammy Esteves
- *The Social Licence to Operate: Your Management Framework for Complex Times* Leeora Black

- *Building a Sustainable Supply Chain*   Gareth Kane

- *Management Systems for Sustainability: How to Successfully Connect Strategy and Action*   Phil Cumming

- *Understanding Integrated Reporting: The Concise Guide to Integrated Thinking and the Future of Corporate Reporting*   Carol Adams

Subscriptions

In addition to individual sales of our ebooks, we now offer subscriptions. Access 60+ ebooks for the price of 5 with a personal subscription to our full e-library. Institutional subscriptions are also available for your staff or students. Visit **www.dosustainability.com/books/subscriptions** or email **veruschka@dosustainability.com**

Write for us, or suggest a DōShort

Please visit **www.dosustainability.com** for our full publishing programme. If you don't find what you need, write for us! Or suggest a DōShort on our website. We look forward to hearing from you.

Abstract

IF YOUR COMPANY HAS AN AMBITIOUS SET of sustainability goals, you'll already know that they can't be achieved from the safety of global headquarters. Change needs to be driven locally, taking into account the priorities, environment and culture of each business area. But how can you achieve this when you can't be everywhere at once?

What you need is a network: a small army of people from across the business who know their department, country or brand inside out, and who can find the right way to create sustainable change that sticks.

When you've spent a long time persuading senior management that the sustainability agenda is business-critical, it's difficult to place the delivery of your precious goals in the hands of others, outsourcing control but retaining accountability.

Networks for Sustainability gives you the tools to review and improve your sustainability network, whether you're revitalising a jaded group of champions or setting up your network from scratch.

It covers all stages of network development, including making the business case, choosing and appointing the right people, and getting the best out of your champions.

....

About the Author

SARAH HOLLOWAY is an independent consultant in sustainability strategy and communications. She specialises in supporting sustainability professionals through the tricky process of creating real, lasting change within their organisations. She has held senior sustainability roles at Unilever, Tesco and TUI Travel, working on sustainability strategy, policies, reporting, consumer and employee engagement – and, of course, leading global networks of sustainability champions. She started her career as a director of sustainability communications agency Futerra, where she worked with clients in the energy, telecommunications and beauty industries. Sarah studied Human Sciences at the University of Oxford and holds an MProf in Leadership for Sustainable Development from Forum for the Future.

Acknowledgments

I'M SINCERELY GRATEFUL to Kylie Bowen, Rosie Bristow, Eileen Donnelly and Toby Radcliffe for sharing their stories about their own sustainability networks. Huge thanks to Theo Holloway and Anne-Christina Hitchin for helping me make sense of it all. . . and extra special thanks to Lyra for all the interruptions.

Contents

CHAPTER 1

Introduction

WE ALL AGREE ON THE BASICS that are needed to get a sustainability strategy off the ground. Support from the board? Essential. Engagement with key stakeholders? Crucial. Ambitious sustainability goals, with clear metrics? Wouldn't be without them.

When the conversation turns to delivery of those goals, things get more interesting. In small companies, or those in which sustainability is relatively new, the sustainability team (or person) often soldiers on alone, delivering what they can with any resource they can beg, borrow or steal. In more advanced organisations, there are nearly always several people from different departments working on specific sustainability impacts and opportunities.

Sometimes, though, I meet a different kind of sustainability manager: one who actively wants to go it alone. When I ask about their internal network – the people they rely on to deliver their goals – they say with pride, 'Oh no, we don't have sustainability champions here. At company X, we believe' – and here they adopt an earnest expression – 'we believe that sustainability is *everyone's* job.'

To which I say: come off it. (That's not quite true; but what I actually say isn't fit for publication.) I know you think a statement like that makes you sound ahead of the pack, but that's just not true. Any company with truly transformative sustainability goals knows that delivering them requires specific changes to parts of the company that can only be achieved with tenacity, local knowledge and, yes, dedicated resources. Claiming that sustainability is 'everyone's job' is the same thing as saying it's no-one's job.

(Inevitably, later in the conversation they'll tell me that 'sustainability is in our company's DNA'. That's the point at which I usually excuse myself, find a quiet corner, and have a little cry.)

If you genuinely think you're going to transform an entire company by yourself, my advice would be to put down this book and walk away. Far from being a point of pride, lack of a network is an admission that you haven't grasped the scale of the challenge presented by the sustainability challenges of the twenty-first century.

Why read this book?

Creating and developing a network of sustainability champions is difficult – we all know that. What you may not appreciate is that one of the biggest barriers may well be you, the network lead. When you've spent months (or years, or possibly even decades) persuading senior management that the sustainability agenda is business-critical, it's difficult to countenance placing the delivery of your precious goals in the hands of others, outsourcing control but retaining accountability.

I understand and sympathise. I've been a network lead myself, more than once, and supported others in the same role. Much of the content of this book is based on my own experience, which includes a respectable number of mistakes.

Although this guidance is not specific to any one culture or type of business, I must admit to a bias towards large organisations, and those headquartered in the UK, because that's where the bulk of my experience lies. I've also worked extensively with networks of what I call 'general sustainability champions' (see page 16) and although I believe that many of the lessons are true for other contexts, you're best placed to judge what will work for you.

This book is unashamedly focused on 'soft skills': how to work with a network of people in different areas of the organisation, with varying levels of knowledge, enthusiasm and commitment to sustainability. Those who over- and under-promise, and those whose delivery can be relied upon like clockwork. Those who are in thrall to their manager or don't get on with them at all, and those who have wonderful relationships with all their stakeholders.

Your ambitious sustainability goals must be delivered no matter who's involved, and you need the skills, mindset and game plan to make sure that happens. This book will show you how.
....

CHAPTER 2

Getting the Basics Right

DO YOU REMEMBER THE 'GREEN POLICE'? Those champions of all things environmental who harangued colleagues about the power settings on their computers, kept an eye out for rogue single-sided printing, and interrogated visitors about their transport arrangements? (You'll definitely remember them if you ever tried to arrive for a meeting by car.)

Too many of us have had brushes with the 'old' type of sustainability champion, put in place when corporate responsibility was all about changing small behaviours in the office. Those champions had their place – but now that sustainability is about transforming the business, it's time for a new type of champion: one who has a good understanding of the sustainability agenda, who knows how to influence and inspire, and who is empowered to make real decisions.

These are the people I'm talking about when I refer to 'sustainability champions'.

An important note: Although 'champion' is a good catch-all name for the members of your network, it doesn't make a great job title for the champions themselves. In Europe and North America, and possibly further, 'champion' has a low-status feel to it (see page 49 for why this is a bad idea). If your champions are full-time and you have any say in their job titles, consider Sustainability Manager, Coordinator or Lead rather than Sustainability Champion.

The four types of sustainability network

Like new students at Hogwarts, sustainability networks are split into four main types. If you're in a large global organisation with truly transformative sustainability goals, you'll need more than one type of network to achieve them.

1. General sustainability champions

General champions own your sustainability strategy in their area of the business – whether that's a country, region, department, brand or product. Their role is to interpret the strategy and goals to form a local sustainability plan, gain the buy-in of senior management, and oversee the delivery of the plan through their own network of contacts and specialists. They often take responsibility for internal communications on sustainability, stakeholder engagement, reporting, and sometimes also marketing and other external communications.

General sustainability champions are *change agents*, and need the skills to match.

TUI Travel's Global Sustainability Coordinators

The 16 people who manage the delivery of TUI Travel's sustainability commitments are a diverse group. Around three-quarters have taken on full-time roles as coordinators, and the rest combine their champion responsibilities with another role, usually 50:50.

The part-time roles are often to be found in internal communications,

---

but the network also includes a finance director and a business manager.

Network lead Kylie Bowen, Group Sustainability Planning and Communications Manager, doesn't mind that the coordinators are a varied bunch. 'In many ways, the variety of jobs means that the group is stronger, because we have a range of perspectives. It's all about what is appropriate for the market or department. We've found that a coordinator's day-to-day role doesn't matter as much as their ability to get the job done: to influence and inspire others, and achieve their targets.

'The only thing to be aware of is that having a second role means they may find certain elements of the champion responsibilities easier than others. For an internal communications manager, for example, engaging employees will be second nature, but implementing the Travelife [hotel sustainability certification] system will not. They'll need more support in these areas.'

2. Functional champions

Functional champions are specialists who oversee a limited number of goals within their specialism: usually those which require similar efforts in most business areas.

Energy efficiency, packaging reduction and sustainability communications are prime examples of goals that benefit from functional networks, because much of the work can be translated from country to country, or across different brands.

Functional champions are *delivery agents* rather than change agents, because they deliver against specific parameters and are not usually called upon to make complex decisions.

Functional networks have two main needs:

- **Specific, measurable goals** and clear guidelines for their achievement. For example, the facilities managers of your offices might have five key tasks to perform that will meet your targets for energy, water and paper reduction.

- **A strong network lead.** Functional champions are specialists, and are primed to listen only to other specialists. Don't try to lead a functional network if you don't know the technical side of the job inside out – instead, appoint someone else from within their field.

TUI UK & Ireland's Retail champions

TUI UK & Ireland has 30 Retail Sustainability Champions – store managers from across the country who oversee sustainability activities in their region.

Their role is to ensure that all retail staff can talk to customers about greener and fairer holidays, and to achieve specific targets on customer donations to the World Care Fund, which supports sustainable tourism projects.

The network was created by a senior manager in the Retail department, who was given sustainability as a management development project. Champions were appointed by their Regional Managers, and the network is led from within Retail.

Rosie Bristow, Sustainability Planning and Communications Manager, supports the network lead from within the TUI UK & Ireland sustainability team.

'We had wanted to set up a sustainability network in Retail for a long time, but the idea didn't get traction until the recommendation came – independently – from inside the department.

'It's important that the network is led by a specialist in Retail. It means the champions see it as something that's part of the way we work – and since the retail teams work in such a specific way, they know exactly what will motivate the champions to achieve. We in the sustainability team contribute enough knowledge and the right tools to allow them to "own" sustainability. It works really well for us.'

3. Sponsor networks

All sustainability teams should have a network of senior-level contacts throughout the business who help to craft and embed the right policies and processes for sustainability. These contacts are crucial for delivery of goals, giving insights into different areas of the business and opening doors to change.

Many businesses formalise this network into a sustainability committee, which meets regularly and forms part of the governance of the sustainability strategy. Others prefer to leave their senior contacts as an informal network of sponsors for specific projects or general sustainability champions (see above).

Much of the advice in this book applies to your network of senior sponsors, particularly chapter 5 on defining your relationship with champions. But because they are more senior and can make or break parts of your strategy, you'll need to make sure you communicate with your sponsors on a one-to-one basis, rather than as a group.

If you're keen to find out more, there's plenty of brilliant advice on how to identify, approach and nurture your key contacts so that you can deliver your goals. My favourite is another DōShort, *The First 100 Days on the Job* by Anne Augustine.

Virgin Group's informal network of sponsors

Eileen Donnelly ran Virgin Group's sustainability network for six years.

'Because Virgin's brands are so diverse, and because the Group's management style was very "light touch", it didn't make sense for us to have a sustainability network in the formal sense. But, as Group Head of Sustainability, it was absolutely crucial that I had good relationships with key brands and departments.

'The right contact for each brand was always someone different from the last, and often not the person I first thought it would be. For example, Virgin Active, our health and fitness brand, had a community investment manager in place – but we identified that their main sustainability impact was in energy, so the UK Energy Manager became my regular contact in the business.

'I found that the most important element of interacting with such a diverse group of people was tailoring what I said to each of them. Each champion needs help understanding why the conversation you're having is relevant to *their* world – as opposed to *your* world – and that can take a long time, with a lot of give and take, listening and talking.

'I always tried to step into their world with them, not ask them to join me in mine.'

4. Employee champions

Finally, many organisations run groups of employee champions whose role it is to inspire and motivate their colleagues to change specific behaviours related to sustainability. Their role might be to encourage recycling in offices or energy reduction in factories, to gather ideas for the next marketing campaign, or to raise funds for the corporate charity.

Employee champions tend to be volunteers rather than strategic appointees, and they're best thought of as part of *employee engagement* rather than change management.

The people who volunteer for employee champion roles are enthusiastic and dedicated, and it's important to channel those qualities into positive action. Occasionally, employee champions can misunderstand their role – remember the 'green police' from the beginning of this chapter? – which, it goes without saying, can only harm the reputation of your team.

So if you're going to have an employee network, it needs to be resourced properly. You'll need training, targets, managerial signoff, communications materials, advice, a buddy system for new champions – in short, much more than many network leads realise. But, done well, employee champions can be an extremely effective communications channel, promoting visibility of your programme and helping others to get involved.

Several authors have outlined the best approach to managing employee champions. A good starting point is the Doughty Centre's *Corporate Responsibility Champions Network: A 'How to' Guide.*[1]

EDF Energy's Company Makers

As a supporter of London 2012, EDF Energy was in the perfect position to appreciate the success of the Games Makers – the 70,000 volunteers who made the Olympic Games happen – and decided to refresh the company's employee volunteering programme around the same theme.

The EDF Energy Company Makers were launched in late 2012, offering employees the opportunity to get involved in specific activities around the company's sustainability commitments.

Toby Radcliffe, Sustainability Culture Manager at EDF Energy, oversees the Company Makers, ensuring their activities align with the company's sustainability strategy.

'By bringing together the different types of champion we already had – for example, environmental ambassadors, diversity champions and education volunteers – into one network, and refocusing them on our company ambitions, we're using our resources much more effectively and learning from the best practice that already existed in the networks.

'Company Makers are a valuable resource for making sure everyone knows about sustainability at EDF Energy, and feels some ownership of it. Volunteers also learn new skills, get training and get to do something a little bit different at work – so everybody wins!'

The benefits of having a network

At some point, you'll need to prepare a business case for creating or maintaining your sustainability network(s). At its most basic, the business case is simple. You need champions for the same reason you need any sort of employee: the job to be done requires additional resource, and you want to bring the best people on board.

But you may find your managers need a little more than that, so here's a run-down of the biggest benefits of having a sustainability network.

Cost-effectiveness

Sustainability teams are under a lot of pressure. Not only are they expected to deliver against a challenging set of goals, they have to do so with little formal resource. A network of champions is one of the most cost-effective ways of mobilising people across the business without landing the full expense in one department's budget.

Translation

An effective sustainability network is made up of champions who know their area of the business inside out. This allows them to 'translate' the global sustainability strategy to their area, making it relevant to senior management and their colleagues. Translation is crucial for the success of your strategy, because the most important sustainability issues vary by country, department and brand – and so does the company culture, pace of work and approach to change.

Your champions also provide a translation service in the other direction: from local to global. A 2009 study by the Doughty Centre[2] found this to be a critical function of sustainability champions. In the words of one of its interviewees: 'The champion is the point of contact locally, listening from the bottom up. . . our finger is on the pulse of reality of what the business needs.'

Visibility and profile

The employees of corporations can be a cynical bunch, and often with good reason. New initiatives seem to come and go with the seasons, disappearing as fast as they materialised, and regenerating a few years later like an unwelcome corporate Doctor Who.

In that environment, your colleagues could be forgiven for suspecting that your sustainability strategy is not to be taken seriously. The sustainability network is a vital tool to combat their suspicion.

Researchers David Cantor, Paula Morrow and Frank Montabon[3] studied employees in the supply chain division of a global retailer. They measured the impact that perceptions of the company's commitment to sustainability had on employees' own commitment to the firm's environmental goals. Unsurprisingly, the more employees believed the firm was committed to a goal, the more they responded with increased effort to achieve it.

In other words, your colleagues know that an under-resourced strategy won't succeed, and they won't risk their own reputation in support of an initiative they believe will fail. A well-resourced, senior-level sustainability sponsor and champion in each business area is the best way to demonstrate that the company is truly committed to sustainability.

Human distance

Although many companies place significant stock in the 'loyalty' of their employees, the truth is that most people are not predisposed to feel loyal to a corporation. In contrast, they are often extremely committed to their colleagues and immediate team.

Cantor *et al.* found that the employees who work hardest to achieve environmental goals are the ones who believe they matter to those around them: '. . .while employees may trust the CEO, they pay closest attention to their peers and immediate manager for both information and advice'.

Even in global companies, human distance still matters. If you want employees to change the way they work, the person asking them needs to be 'like them' – in the same country, working to promote the same brand, or with the same specialism – and to understand what makes them tick.

Choosing your network

Hopefully, you'll already have worked out which network – or combination of networks – is right for you. In many cases, setting them up involves a series of obvious choices. If you're setting up a functional network to save energy in your offices, the champions will be the facilities managers, and they'll have clear targets and actions. Likewise, if you want to embed sustainability criteria into performance development, you need a senior sponsor from the HR department who can identify the best way to do this.

It's the general sustainability champions who are trickiest to manage. Since they look after the full range of sustainability initiatives in their business area, it's not always immediately obvious who the champions should be, how the network should be structured, and how best to deliver your sustainability goals while making the role a fulfilling one for the champions.

So for the rest of this book, we're going to look at general sustainability networks specifically. Don't worry if your network is of a different type. Many (if not all) of the lessons learned here are applicable to functional, sponsor and employee networks as well.

....

CHAPTER 3

Setting the Right Strategy

IN REALITY, YOU'RE UNLIKELY TO FIND yourself setting up a network from scratch. Unless you're the very first person to consider the future of your company in light of environmental limits and the values of society, there are almost certainly other employees dealing with sustainability issues as part of their day jobs. Let's call these people your 'contacts'.

That means you already have the raw materials for your network. As network lead, your role is to formalise their role as champions, and bring structure and direction to their work. (You'll find more on the role of network lead in chapter 4).

When to set up a network

When's the best time to start transforming your contacts into a living, breathing network? Probably earlier than you think.

It's tempting to see network development as a job to be done once you've completed your sustainability strategy, complete with key performance indicators and annual targets. After all, that's when you'll be clear on exactly what you want them to do.

That's a perfectly reasonable way of doing things, and many companies take this approach. But I'd strongly recommend that you think more carefully about the timing of your network's development. Ideally, your network of sustainability managers should be forming *as you formulate your company's sustainability strategy*. They should be there with you as you gather the data, have their say on the company's priorities, and feed back on your plans for delivery.

It's well worth bringing key people on board while your thoughts are still forming, for the following reasons:

- **Your strategy will be more robust.** You need your contacts' involvement in strategy setting for the same reason you need them for delivery: they have local (country, department or brand) knowledge that you do not. This local knowledge can mean the difference between a great-sounding goal, and one that actually works.

- **You can test your relationship.** When you involve your contacts in setting your goals, you're not yet appointing them as official network champions. You're getting to know them and building mutual trust. This is your opportunity to find out whether they would make the right champions for the delivery of your goals.

- **Champions will respect your goals.** Research from Harvard Business School shows that goal-setting can induce unethical behaviour – people 'gaming' the system – particularly if they are not involved in setting the goals.[4] Where objectives are imposed from above, they tend to narrow our focus and make us forget the reason they were set; but involving your network early means they will understand the context, and will be committed to delivering your goals for the right reasons.

How you include them is up to you. I've found that workshops of key contacts are a fruitful way of gathering input and forming goals. If you think this is just good stakeholder engagement, you're right. But a smart sustainability team will be looking at their contacts not just as stakeholders, but as a potential future project team.

Setting a strategy with your network in mind

The right strategy – and how you go about developing it – very much depends on your company. But there are certain elements that you can incorporate that will make it easier for your sustainability champions to interpret, build on and deliver your strategy.

1. Clear links with business strategy

The biggest gift you can give your champions is a sustainability strategy that is closely linked to the core strategy of your business. This is best practice, of course, and leading companies such as Unilever, Marks & Spencer and Patagonia have attempted to go one step beyond this, to develop sustainable business models, providing us with a glimpse of what can be achieved when the mindset of 'achieving sustainability goals' gives way to that of 'becoming a sustainable business'.

Your company may not yet be at that stage. But if you're working against the core strategy, you'll soon find that gaining traction is more difficult at every level of the organisation. The impact on sustainability champions is particularly severe, because they are a long way from the global sustainability team and its clear business case.

If your sustainability strategy is at odds with your business strategy, I'd advise you to postpone your plans for a network, and focus instead on working with senior management to bring them closer together. You'll need to identify how current and future environmental, economic and social challenges will affect your business strategy, and how you can build a sustainability strategy that will deliver business advantage.

2. Clear, data-driven global goals

Global goals provide a true north for all your sustainability champions' activities. In order to help champions deliver them effectively, two attributes are particularly important: they need to be *clear* and *data-driven*.

For example: *Reduce carbon dioxide equivalent emissions from major premises (top 50 offices) by 30% per square foot by 2015, against a baseline of 2012.*

Why is it clear? It has a baseline (2012), a due date (2015), a specific scope (top 50 offices), a target (30% reduction per square foot) and a clear metric (carbon dioxide equivalent emissions). That means it's pretty difficult to massage the figures: either it will be achieved or it won't be.

Why is it data-driven? Because this goal has a baseline, which means there are good data to show where we are now. To help champions reduce emissions in their business area, you would give them the baseline data for the appropriate office buildings, along with guidance to help them decide how the reduction can best be achieved.

3. Flexibility and autonomy of delivery

No matter how global your goals, the delivery of your sustainability strategy will always be local. That means that high-quality insight into local values, consumer behaviours and stakeholder positions is critical – and that champions should be free to deliver those goals in the best way for their business area.

One of the first tasks of a sustainability champion will be to interpret the global strategy for their department, brand or country, and to develop a local sustainability plan. You can help by providing your champions with a clear set of goals, guidance on how to localise them – and, crucially, the data behind those goals. It's the data that allow champions to decide which goals are relevant to their context. See page 60 for more on helping champions define their local plans.

4. Local senior support

We know that the support of senior management is important for your sustainability strategy to thrive – it's the only way your team will have a true mandate to influence change across the business.

For sustainability champions, the key ingredient for success is senior support *within their area of the business*. That means that, alongside your network of champions in key business areas, you'll need to develop a network of senior sponsors to support them. The sponsors are there to ensure sustainability is represented in strategic conversations within the department, brand or country, and to open doors for the champion when they need to connect with key people.

Does that sound familiar? If so, you're right: it's the sponsor network discussed on page 19. Many companies formalise this network into a sustainability committee, which allows for a closer-knit group of senior sponsors to oversee the whole sustainability strategy.

Senior sponsors and sustainability committees are often involved in selecting and appointing champions. See page 51 for more details.

CHAPTER 4

Understanding Your Role

LEADING A NETWORK CAN BE A REAL CHALLENGE. Your role as network lead is unlikely to be a full-time one, and you'll need to judge how much of your time should be spend influencing your champions, as opposed to working with the board, compiling the annual sustainability report, or nurturing new initiatives.

Network leads do not deliver sustainability projects directly. That's a new experience for many of managers, who are used to having direct control over outcomes. It often feels as if everyone else is doing the real work, and it's difficult to see how you make an impact.

If you're managing a global network of champions, it's unlikely you'll be able to meet them more than once or twice a year – and that's if you're lucky. So you'll have to exercise clear leadership skills to ensure your sustainability goals are achieved despite the physical distance.

So how do you lead a network under all these constraints?

Becoming an internal consultant

In business and our personal lives, we tend to have a limited number of roles – parent, teacher, friend, boss – that we fall into very easily. The network lead is none of these things. I should know: I've tried them all on for size, and although in the short term some of them work (for example, 'parenting' a manager through a task), in the long term they all have clear drawbacks.

The role you should be aiming for is that of internal consultant. In *Flawless Consulting*,[5] one of my favourite books on leadership and influencing, Peter Brock gives a description of a consultant that I've found invaluable in guiding my work as a network lead: 'We can be a guide through a process of discovery, engagement, and dialogue in which our clients will find an answer to their question and launch an implementation that will be enduring and productive.'

The challenge is not to deliver a perfectly packaged programme of work, but to support and guide network members in *finding their own answers* to the question of how to implement the sustainability strategy.

What are the implications of being an internal consultant?

1. You start to think like a consultant

Seeing yourself as a consultant helps you to define your relationship with your champions and set a consistent tone and approach. Getting this wrong can have far-reaching consequences.

Let's take two hypothetical examples.

- **Simon** runs a global network of sustainability managers from his head office in New York. He doesn't take much time to think about his relationship with his champions, but if he did, he'd realise he had set up a series of teacher-pupil relationships. Even though he's kind and patient with his pupils, the hierarchy is clear: he's the expert, and the champions deliver his agenda. When one of his champions runs into a problem, he gives detailed advice. If that doesn't work, he just gets it done himself, even if it means extra work.

- **Anna** works in Sydney, but most of her sustainability network is in Europe. She spends a lot of her time on the phone – often out of hours – with her champions, hearing of their struggles to gain traction. Unlike Simon, Anna is very clear about her role: it's to offer support, to engender trust, and to be a friend. Anna finds it difficult to press her champions to act if something isn't going as planned. They do indeed trust her with their problems; they just never seem to be able tackle those problems by themselves.

In both of these cases, it's the *mindset* of the network lead that stops them from providing effective support to their champions. In different ways, they're both encouraging their network to become dependent on them, when they should be building the capacity of their champions to solve their own problems.

2. You define your own boundaries

The real danger of being a network lead is that, because you deliver support rather than results, there's no defined end point to your work. You can always offer more support, create more training programmes, develop more communications materials, and ask for more case studies.

That means *you need to decide where to stop*. You may find you have to define your boundaries more explicitly than you have done in the past. Consultants do this all the time, defining who they work with, when they're available, and what is expected of them. As an internal consultant, you can do that too.

3. You change your attitude towards resistance

A manager fears resistance; a consultant expects it. That's because they understand that all change creates resistance. Some of it is pointless sniping, but the rest is debate that needs to happen. Resistance to ideas is a sign that people are taking the idea seriously – after all, it's easy to agree with something you intend to ignore.

Resistance is key to the consultant–client relationship, so you should expect it in your relationship with your champions. You'll frequently have to make decisions about what to do when you encounter this resistance: whether to push harder, or to let go. For more on resistance, see chapter 9.

4. You accept the limits of your responsibility

As an internal consultant, your job is to build capacity for your clients to solve problems themselves. You're responsible for delivering excellent goals, targets, training and support. . . but you're not responsible for your champions' results.

That's a real departure for lots of corporate managers, so I'll say it again: *you are not responsible for their results*. You are not responsible for their failure to gain buy-in for that critical training, or their long-running argument with the facilities manager that means the carbon data come in late every quarter. You're not even responsible if they launch an external campaign chock-full of dodgy claims about their environmental record (though, in this case, you're likely to be called upon to help repair the damage).

Because no matter what you (or your boss) would like, you cannot force them to do what you say, and nor can you change their basic strengths and weaknesses. All you can do is spot problems arising in good time, support the champion in solving them, or choose to let it (or them) go. That's it.

What's different about an internal consultant?

Most managers are familiar with how to work with external consultants, hired to look at a specific problem, provide recommendations and leave. But we're often less comfortable with the role of an internal consultant.

It's helpful to consider the success of other functions that work in this way – for example, Human Resources. Many companies now refer to their HR managers as Business Partners, acting as internal consultants for specific departments. The best HR departments set out clearly the ways in which their role adds value, what they'll do for the duration of their contract with a manager and, what they expect in return. It's worth seeking out the HR team in your business and quizzing them on how they manage these relationships – you'll gain invaluable insights that are specific to your business.

The bad news is that the role of internal consultant is more challenging than its external counterpart. I'll go back to *Flawless Consulting*[6] to understand why this is:

* **Colleagues know more about you.** 'You have a status and job level that is known to most people in the organization. This can limit your access to key high-level people you should be contacting directly.' If you've worked in the organisation for a while, colleagues will know more than just your status and job level – you're likely

to have had conversations with them before, built rapport and traded favours. Whether that's a good or bad thing depends on how you've behaved in the past.

- **Clients often don't choose to work with you.** HR teams are the experts on this problem. They offer a service to their departments which they believe adds real value – but often they're seen as a barrier to getting things done. External consultants can let difficult clients go and move on, but that's more difficult internally: if your difficult client works for a key department, you may have to persevere with the relationship despite its challenges.

- **It's hard to say 'no'.** You might feel you can't refuse a request for support from a champion, especially if they are senior or a refusal might impact on your career trajectory.

- **You also have to judge how well they're doing.** You not only advise on the way forward, as a consultant would, but you're responsible for judging and reviewing the success of the results. That means you don't have the luxury of railing against the demands of 'management' with your client – because you *are* management.

An external consultant needs to pitch for work, submit a proposal, negotiate a contract with specific deliverables, and account for their delivery – and will almost certainly incur a financial penalty if the deliverables are not met.

I'd encourage you to try to observe as many of the formal aspects of the consultant–client relationship as possible. Depending on the culture of your workplace, that might be all of them, or just the one or two that you think are most important. At the very least, an email setting out how you've agreed to work together, and what each of you will do, shouldn't disturb even the most laidback of corporate cultures.

The skills you need

A recent study from Weinreb Consulting and Net Impact found that interpersonal skills were the most important attribute a sustainability professional must have to be successful. In their survey of new corporate sustainability leads, the majority (78%) said that subject matter expertise would be the greatest predictor of success. Once on the job, however, *all* respondents said interpersonal skills proved to be the most critical.

Attributes of a CR network lead[7]

The Doughty Centre identified several attributes of a good CR (corporate responsibility) lead:

- True passion for CR and ability to stay updated on trends and stakeholder viewpoints

- Heavyweight relationship managers, good at persuading, influencing and inspiring

- Skilled change managers

- Enablers, not micro-managers. This involves a degree of risk taking and trust-building skills

- Good insight into the business – understanding how the CR philosophy integrates into the business strategy, with a strong business focus on CR

You may already have your own list of the skills you need to be a good network lead. Mine would include: authenticity, fairness, tenacity, cultural sensitivity, empathy and listening skills, the ability to prioritise and knowledge of how things work in the company.

There are two that are worth talking about in more detail.

1. Prioritisation

Sustainability teams are asked to achieve transformative results, often with less resource than their colleagues in other functions. Chances are, you already have a lot on your plate even without a network to look after. But you can't be everywhere at once, and you can't help everyone.

There are two angles to consider when you're prioritising your work with champions:

- **Prioritise your attention within the network.** Your time is finite and precious, so you need to ask some tough questions. Which projects are the most critical? Which are most likely to need your support? Which champions are most likely to need your support? Once you're clear about your priority champions, you can feel confident about declining other requests for help.

- **Make the network part of your other work.** You'll need to be realistic about how much time you spend with the network and how much on other aspects of your role. But remember that the network is a delivery mechanism, not just another project. Can the network help you to deliver your other projects, so that time spent on champions helps the rest of your workload?

NETWORKS FOR SUSTAINABILITY:
HARNESSING PEOPLE POWER TO DELIVER YOUR GOALS

2. Empathy

Empathy is the management buzzword of the past few years – it seems as if you can't move for articles on the 'habits of empathetic people' and exhortations to 'manage with empathy'. But there's a reason for that. In the modern economy, where employees increasingly seek not only financial reward but also fulfilment, empathy is a key skill for all managers.

Nowhere is this exemplified better than in sustainability. The changes required in a sustainability programme go to the heart of how the business works, changing habits that have been there nearly a lifetime for some people, and requiring that we take risks to innovate and change the way we work.

There's little space in this short book to explore the role of empathy in detail, so instead I recommend you look up Brené Brown, who has written extensively on the subject. A good place to start is her TED Talk on 'The Power of Vulnerability'.[8]

....

CHAPTER 5

Choosing the Right People

YOUR SUSTAINABILITY CHAMPIONS EXIST to deliver your ambitious sustainability goals, and they're also the public face of your sustainability strategy. Clearly, finding... the right people is an important step in achieving your goals.

But it's unlikely you'll have total control over who becomes a champion, and it's in the nature of business (with its changing priorities, uncertain resources and constant moving of people) that you won't ever assemble the perfect team. You're much more likely to find yourself with a diverse set of champions at different levels of the business, with their own specialisms and varying capacity to undertake sustainability tasks. That means that part of your role as network lead will be to smooth over the creases, making the delivery appear seamless for the purposes of reporting and communications.

The champion role

The role of sustainability champion is difficult. Your champions are change agents in the 'real world' outside global headquarters. They'll be up against the daily grind of financial targets, competing business agendas and colleagues who are suspicious of this new 'sustainability' thing.

Exactly what you want your champions to do will, of course, depend on your context. Here's my own list of tasks, based on my experience. Please take the elements that speak to you, ignore the rest, and add in for yourself anything I've missed.

There are three areas to cover:

1. Strategy

Champions should define the problem (the sustainability priorities for their business area) and plan the solution (their own local sustainability plan). Specifically, they should:

- **Develop a local version of the sustainability strategy**, based on the global strategy and their local insight, with clear goals for their business area and annual targets against them.

- **Manage local internal stakeholders**, reporting to senior management in their business area and developing a support network of their own.

2. Delivery

Champions will deliver against the goals in their local sustainability plan. In most cases, this will include communications and stakeholder engagement. Key tasks include to:

- **Manage local projects** and oversee local contributions to global projects, holding others accountable for delivery.

- **Make sustainability real for colleagues** through internal communication of local sustainability issues and projects.

- **Manage local external stakeholders** – for example, government and NGOs.

- **Develop their own influencing network** of key people to get things done.

3. Evaluation

Champions should assess whether the local sustainability plan is working (delivering results in a way that supports the global goals), and make adjustments where necessary. They will also need to support the company's sustainability reporting process.

- **Report back** to you (the network lead) and their fellow champions regularly, completing a sustainability scorecard if required.

- **Provide data and access to key people** for the annual sustainability report.

- **Oversee measurement of global targets** in their business area if appropriate (e.g. follow up with key people in other networks).

- Work with sustainability champions in other business areas to share best practice and support each other.

Full-time versus part-time

In practical terms, one of the most important decisions you'll need to make is whether your champions are full-time or part-time. Your instinct might be to secure full-time resource as quickly as possible, but in fact there are pros and cons for each approach.

	Pros	Cons
Full-time champions	• Champions have no competing work tasks or objectives • Your strategy will have real visibility and clearly allocated resource	• If you can't demonstrate value added for a full-time role, you risk losing them altogether • They are harder to get signed off
Part-time champions	• Their other work can lend legitimacy to their sustainability objectives • They may gain senior level signoff more easily • Some excellent candidates might be happier to combine sustainability with another role • You can have a bigger network with the same budget	• They have other priorities – and sustainability may not come first • The role may seem temporary and less 'official' if it's combined with another role

For many network leads, this decision will be made for you by circumstance and the resources available. It may not be practical, politically expedient or financially viable for you to secure full-time people for your network, even if you'd like them.

Most sustainability networks start off with part-time champions, progressing to full-time roles when the network has shown added value and there is a clear business need for more time to be spent driving change. Most networks will always have a mixture of part-time and full-time champions, depending on the nature of the role in different parts of the business.

How to choose your champions

There are several criteria you'll want to take into account when choosing the right people for your network: seniority, skills, their current role, their values and their personality. The culture of your company – 'the way things are done around here' – should be the driving force behind your decisions.

For the sake of simplicity, it's tempting to decide that champions should be appointed according to role: for example, that you'll ask for 50% of the time of each country's internal communications manager to be dedicated to sustainability. I'd counsel against this, because I think other attributes (particularly influencing skills) are more important. Some internal communications managers will have the enthusiasm, skills and commitment to get the job done; but others will not, and you'll spend a disproportionate amount of time persuading them to commit to the champion role.

I'd recommend you make a simple list of qualities you want in your champions, and look at all available options in light of these qualities. Try and keep it to four or five points – this isn't a job description, but your take on the 'right people' for your network.

Personal traits of a CR champion

The Doughty Centre[9] identified several personal traits for a CR (corporate responsibility) champion:

- a passion for CR;

- interest in the external view;

- building relationships;

- influencers and persuaders;

- 'ability to make it personal';

- change agents, facilitators, networkers and communicators.

If I were looking to appoint a network of champions, my job description would be: *An ambitious senior manager or director with a passion for sustainability, linked clearly to the business, and the ability to inspire and influence others.*

Here's the thinking behind it:

1. Ambitious senior manager or director

Appointing champions at the right level of seniority is crucial in most business cultures, and I've found that the right level is often is director or senior manager.

If your champions are too junior, they won't be able to leverage the changes you need; they're also more likely to change roles frequently at the beginning of their career, meaning you have to start again with a new champion more often.

If your champions are too senior, they won't have time to do the day-to-day work of influencing, persuading and reporting that the role requires. Practically, they're likely to appoint someone in their team (probably a director or senior manager!) to do the real work – turning your 'champion' into a middle man. If this happens, it's best to turn your original champion into the senior sponsor (see page 19).

2. Passion for sustainability, linked clearly to the business

Most emerging sustainability networks are based on 'coalitions of the willing' – employees with the enthusiasm to take on the additional role of champion. But a passion for sustainability, although it's necessary, is not sufficient to make a good champion. They need to be able to link that passion to a commercial business case for sustainability, and to have the right personality and skills to influence others.

3. Ability to inspire and influence others

'Influencing skills' are some of the most sought-after capabilities in business, and it's not difficult to see why. Passion, technical knowledge and seniority won't help your champion fulfil their change management role if they can't influence and inspire others. You should look for people who already have a good network of contacts in their business area – and beyond.

If you're recruiting a country sustainability champion, they should be what *Harvard Business Review*[10] calls a 'cultural connector' – someone who can adapt behaviour across cultural settings and diagnose the degree of adjustment necessary for success. In other words, your champion needs to be a good enough translator to inspire their own business area with a strategy that was designed elsewhere.

Attracting the right people

Whatever your own list of qualities, you need to make sure not only that you've defined the 'right people' for your champion roles, but that you can attract those people to the role. Ambitious people in your business will be choosing from a range of next career steps and, ideally, the sustainability champion role should be among them.

Prospective champions need to know they can trust you, the network lead, so it's always a good idea to be introduced by someone who can vouch for your good work. They also need to be clear on what they'll get out of the relationship. There are lots of benefits to being a champion, and they fall into two broad categories: career progression and the opportunity to live their values at work.

1. Career progression

The collaborative way of working favoured in sustainability is fast becoming a key skill for other business areas. That means that the skills a champion could hope to develop or improve on – influencing, networking, change management – will help them to secure other, more senior roles in the future.

If you can offer access to an international network of champions – and, with it, the prospect of networking their way into a role in another country – this will be a real plus point for potential champions.

In short, if you want to attract high-calibre people, the champion role as high-status as you possibly can.

Linking the champion role to career development

At TUI UK & Ireland, the sustainability champion role is accelerating the career development of shop managers.

'We have lots of shop managers but limited opportunities for promotion above that role,' explains Rosie Bristow, sustainability support to the network of Retail Sustainability Champions. 'That means that the business has identified several options for store managers to take on additional responsibilities and show they are ready for promotion – and becoming a sustainability champion is one of those options.

'It means that becoming a sustainability champion is seen as a real win-win: we get help promoting what we're doing in our shops, and managers see a clear benefit to their career. And it also means they're great at delivering, because the role is part of a formal development process that's being tracked.'

---

2. Living their values at work

Don't underestimate the attraction of an opportunity to 'give back', 'do good' or 'make a difference'. Although these are trite ways of putting it, the truth is that many people feel a disconnect between the person they are expected to be at work and the person they are in the rest of their lives. You're offering an opportunity to bring these two things closer together, and work on something that really matters. Even those who you wouldn't immediately identify as 'values-based' people are likely to be motivated by this – so use it!

Elite versus exclusive

Toby Radcliffe, a network lead of EDF Energy's Company Makers, cites four benefits for champions: skills, training, career progression and 'the opportunity to do something a bit different'.

He also sees the value of making the champion role a high status proposition. 'It's a volunteer role, so there's a limit to what we can do. But we're putting in place simple strategies – things like recognition, access to senior managers and core skills development – to try and make being a Company Maker an elite role.

'In previous years, we didn't invest as much in our volunteers, and the tasks they were given could be fairly menial. Now we offer a range of high-profile activities, all focused on our company ambitions and sustainability goals, which in turn require us to offer quality training and capacity building to prepare our volunteers for their task roles.

'The result is a network that is elite without being exclusive – just where we want to be.'

Appointing champions through sponsors

All of the guidance above is based on a rather shaky assumption: that you have control over the people who are appointed as champions. If you have a sustainability committee (or an informal network of senior sponsors), one of the best ways to ensure champions are well supported is to invite them to appoint champions from within their department, country or brand.

There are pros and cons to this approach: you may have much less control over the people who are appointed, but senior sponsorship adds to the status of the role, and you'll know that they already have a good relationship with their local senior management.

Some of my best champions were appointed in this way, even though a few of them weren't necessarily the people I would have chosen myself. We all tend to favour people who are like us, and appointing them through sponsors ensures a more diverse team – and, usually, champions who are better in tune with the specific needs of their business area.

Inheriting a network

The other situation in which you have little say in champion appointments is when you inherit a network. If you're lucky, your network will already be made up of great champions – but if you're planning to make big changes, you may find that the current champions are no longer the best people for the new one.

Bear in mind that you represent an unknown quantity to your champions, and they'll be looking to judge whether you can be trusted and relied upon. When you meet the champions, resist the temptation to tell them all about your grand plans for the network. Ask them two questions: 'What are you doing?' and 'How can I help?' – and then *listen*.

Once you've gathered all your information and are beginning to make changes to the way the network operates, you should expect some resistance. The best way to combat this is to emphasise what these changes mean: that their work has become more important to the company and that they will play a central role in delivering a key part of business strategy.

What happens if you're sure that one or more of your champions is completely wrong for the network? You need to make a decision: either you work on turning them into suitable champions, or you find a new champion. Only you can decide the best way forward. . . but it's worth bearing in mind this clear message from Apple's Dan Jacobs: 'It's better to have a hole in your team than an asshole in your team!'

....

CHAPTER 6

Starting as You Mean to Go On

THE BEGINNING OF YOUR RELATIONSHIP with your champions sets the tone for the rest of your tenure as their network lead. It's here that you set expectations – of you and of your champions – and agree the goals and workplan you will follow.

Contracting

You know your global sustainability strategy inside out – the business case, the goals, and the plan of how to get there – but your champions don't; not yet. Throw in a few cultural differences (and variations in business culture across departments) and it's clear that you need a starting point for your relationship with a champion. This process is called contracting.

In a traditional consultant–client relationship, there are clear steps in the contracting process: usually an initial meeting, followed by a proposal, feedback and revision of the proposal, and a written contract based on the agreed process. For internal networks, the goals are the same, but in my experience, the process is slightly different. I've identified four steps, which I'll explain over the next few pages.

Before we get into them, let's answer two key questions.

How long will the contracting process take?

Depending on the champion and their particular challenges, these steps might take anything from a couple of weeks to several months. Your champion might need a second meeting to help them understand key issues for their business area; or they might need you to bring a senior member of the global team to meet the local board. If their area of the business is particularly complicated, they might require extra data or support in working out their priorities and targets.

If it's absolutely vital to your business that the champions begin to produce results straight away (and in some cultures this really is true), help them to identify some 'quick wins' that they can deliver alongside the development of the long-term strategy.

What if I'm too late?

It's never too late to set expectations on ways of working, the role of the champions, or the way you report on what you do. In fact, you should revisit these issues regularly to check that everything is still running smoothly. Developing and maintaining a network is a collaborative process, and you and the champions will learn as you go along the best way to make it work.

STEP 1: Do your homework

Your first step should be to draft your expectations. What will the champion do? What will you and your team do? How will your relationship work? How will you communicate?

You'll need to create a few documents to guide your thinking. At a minimum, I'd recommend:

- Sustainability champion role and responsibilities

- Your offer

- Ways of working with champions

- Toolkit for developing a local sustainability plan

You should expect to review and amend these documents regularly. They are not meant to be static documents that are signed for compliance and left to gather dust; the whole point of having them is to shape the way you work with your champions.

Sustainability champion role and responsibilities

See page 42 for details of the role you might want champions to play in your network. Try to keep your roles and responsibilities document as short and easy to use as possible. ·

Your offer

All consultants have a core 'offer', the services they provide to clients. I recommend you go through the roles and responsibilities of your champions point by point, and define the support you expect to provide.

Below is a typical 'offer' matrix, using the champion roles and responsibilities defined on page 43. It's worth noting that much of this 'support from the global team' involves access to the other champions. We'll be returning to this on page 85.

	Champion task	Support the global team offers
Strategy	Develop a local sustainability plan, based on the global strategy and their local insight, with clear goals for their business area and annual targets against them	• Global sustainability goals and how they are measured • Key sustainability data for their business area • Guidance on creating smart local goals and annual targets
	Manage local internal stakeholders, reporting to senior management in their business area and developing a support network of their own	• Templates for board presentations, including an overview of the global strategy • Access to examples of best practice • Access to senior people in the global team to present at board meetings if required

	Champion task	Support the global team offers
Delivery	Manage local projects and oversee local contributions to global projects, holding others accountable for delivery	• Clear guidance on actions required for global projects
	Make sustainability real for colleagues through internal communication of local sustainability issues and projects	• Opportunities for internal communication (for example, an annual Green Day) with template materials that champions can use • Access to a databank of employee engagement materials from other champions
	Manage local external stakeholders – for example, government and NGOs	• Access to local public affairs teams for support • Global policies on key 'hot topics'
	Develop their own influencing network of key people to get things done	• Advice on best practice and access to details of other champions' networks

	Champion task	Support the global team offers
Reporting	Report back to you (the network lead) and their fellow champions regularly, completing a sustainability scorecard if required	• Reporting template and timetable (e.g. once per quarter) • Sustainability scorecard and guidance on how to use it • Access to external support for measurement if required
	Provide data and access to key people for the annual sustainability report	• Timetable for reporting • Opportunity to influence the content of the report
	Oversee measurement of global targets in their business area if appropriate (e.g. follow up with key people in other networks)	• Clear guidance on which global targets are applicable to the business area • An up-to-date list of key contacts for other sustainability networks
	Work with sustainability champions in other business areas to share best practice and offer support	• Opportunities for champions to speak often and meet regularly • 'Buddy' champion for new network members

Ways of working with champions

The 'ways of working' document is a simple way of codifying how you and the champions will treat each other. You can live without one of these, but I've always found it a good way to reassure champions from the outset that we'll be working as a team – and as a reminder for me to work collaboratively when I'm tempted to try and control my champions.

This document can cover anything you like. Here are some ideas to get you started:

- Co-create new policies and training materials where appropriate

- Be transparent about the time commitment for all tasks

- Be flexible with deadlines according to need, and transparent about constraints on all sides

- Acknowledge emails within 48 hours

- Raise issues and problems promptly and respectfully

- Hold one-to-one calls between the global team and each champion at least once a quarter

- Deliver a monthly email round-up of activities and deliverables

- Organise (and attend) regular face-to-face meetings of all champions

Toolkit for developing a local sustainability plan

The best way to deliver guidance on your strategy is through a toolkit – a step-by-step guide for champions to set a local sustainability plan against the global goals.

At a minimum, your toolkit should contain:

- Global goals, with metrics and how they are calculated

- Key local data that are relevant to each of the goals (for example, the department's carbon footprint, or the percentage of employees that are local in the champion's country)

- Guidance on setting priorities and setting appropriate local goals

- How to identify and manage local stakeholders

- Rules and guidance for reporting against the metrics

Importantly, you shouldn't present your champions with a perfectly packaged solution. Your role is to provide them with the raw materials, encourage them to commit to finding a solution, and then get out of their way so they can deliver.

STEP 2: Use your first meeting effectively

Many network managers use their first meeting with each champion as an opportunity to tell them about the role, present the priorities for their business area, and make sure they understand the ways of working. I think this meeting is too valuable to spend in that way; there's a much more important job to be done.

I'd recommend you use this time to do two things: help your champion understand the problem you need to solve, and uncover their concerns about being a sustainability champion.

This meeting should be a discussion, not a briefing, which means it's time for them to talk and you to listen. It may be difficult, but you're helping them do something very important: to define for themselves the problem you will solve together. This helps them take ownership of the strategy from the very beginning.

If your champion can't express their concerns at this stage, have no doubt that they will surface later, at a much more awkward stage. . . or that they'll stay buried forever, and you'll find one day that they're not delivering what you need, and you can't work out why.

This kind of feelings-talk goes against the culture of many businesses, and even of some countries. You're likely to find champions who are happy to tell you how they are reacting to your suggestions, and those who would lose their jobs rather than share their feelings with you. Nonetheless, you should still ask the question and give them an opportunity to express any concerns.

Here are some questions to get you started:

- What do you see as the biggest sustainability challenges for your area?

- What's already going on in your area that we should be doing more of?

- What are your reservations about working with us in the global team?

- Is your manager supportive of your role as champion?

- What do senior management think of sustainability?

Of course, if you want to hold a meeting like this, it's crucial that your champion is familiar with the role, your offer, the agreed ways of working and the toolkit *before* the meeting. Sending and following up pre-reads is crucial.

Face to face versus virtual meetings

Where possible, you should meet your champion in person. In a world of videoconferencing and phone calls, it's tempting to meet them virtually – and while that's certainly the way to go later on, I think it's vital that you 'press the flesh' the first time you meet.

You and your champion need to be comfortable asking difficult questions and responding honestly – and that's difficult to do remotely, because we're missing lots of the physical cues we use to assess what someone really means. (This is an issue that you'll need to tackle throughout your relationship, and I address it further on page 67.)

Is it better for you to go them, or for them to come to you? It's really your choice. If you visit them, you'll be able to get a really good grasp of their sustainability challenges, and perhaps even visit existing local projects. On the other hand, if there are several people you'd like them to meet in the global office, they could spend a few days with you and your team to find out more about how you work.

Meeting the other stakeholder in the contract

Do you know the saying 'what interests the boss, fascinates me'? Well, it's true. And while there are sustainability champions who manage to operate without the blessing of their manager, they are few and far between, and their tenure as champion is often limited. So, if at all possible, you should hold an additional meeting with your champion and their manager, together.

Your goal is to persuade the manager that the role of sustainability champion will be a valuable one to have within their team. You can present the global sustainability strategy with an emphasis on its business value and the high esteem in which it's held among senior management, and get the champion to explain the next steps to their manager.

STEP 3: Support their first steps

At the end of your first meeting, you should have agreed a list of next steps for developing the contract between you. Most likely, they will agree to draft the local sustainability plan and sign it off with their own senior management, and you'll agree to confirm the plan and provide reporting tools and guidance.

You can also help them by sharing some powerful techniques for success.

Looking for 'bright spots'

'Bright spots' are the success stories that already exist in their business areas, and they can help to accelerate a local sustainability plan beyond the obvious. As the science fiction author William Gibson once said, 'The future is here; it's just not widely distributed yet.'

Your champions should be looking for their own bright spots. As well as analysing the sustainability challenges, your champions should be asking 'what's already working – and how can we do more of it?' They are likely to find many more practical solutions than by relying on your macro-level data alone.

Using 'bright spots' in Vietnam

In their excellent book *Switch: How To Change Things When Change Is Hard*,[11] Chip and Dan Heath tell the story of Jerry Sternin,

---

a Save The Children team leader who was charged with reducing childhood malnutrition in Vietnam.

Sternin's strategy was an innovative one: instead of looking at the macro trends that led to malnutrition (poverty, water scarcity, lack of nutritional knowledge), his team spent time in local villages finding out what the mothers of well-nourished children were doing differently. In other words, they looked for bright spots.

The team found that the 'bright spot' mothers were following local conventions, but with a few key differences: they were adding small shrimps and sweet potato greens to their children's rice, and were splitting their food into four meals instead of two, making them easier for small bodies to digest.

Sternin recruited local mothers to teach other families how to cook in this way, eventually reaching 2.2 million people in 265 villages. The team's focus on the bright spots rather than macro trends allowed them to find simple solutions that worked within local customs, and made a real difference.

Finding 'godparents'

Your champions will be looking to make changes to their area of the business, and they won't be able to do it without the buy-in of senior people. They should be thinking about when and how to update their senior management on their plans and progress.

In their 2009 report, the Doughty Centre[12] identified another senior stakeholder: the mentor or 'godparent'. They found that effective change

NETWORKS FOR SUSTAINABILITY:
HARNESSING PEOPLE POWER TO DELIVER YOUR GOALS

agents almost always had a senior colleague they went to for advice on how to solve specific problems, how to engage colleagues, or even just for moral support.

Encourage your champions to look not only for their 'official' stakeholders, but also for a mentor who will take a real interest in their personal development and the progress of their local sustainability plan.

STEP 4: Sign the contract

In most cases, you won't need a real, signed contract with your champions. But it is useful to develop a short document, signed off by the champion's senior manager and yours, outlining the local sustainability plan for the business area and including key targets and deliverables. This is the document against which you'll judge whether the business area is making progress on sustainability.

CHAPTER 7

Communicating Effectively

GOOD COMMUNICATION IS THE BACKBONE of managing a network of champions: get the frequency, timing and depth of communication right, and your sustainability goals will be delivered much more smoothly.

From the champion's point of view, clear communications instil confidence that they have all the information they need to deliver, and to update their local senior management. They'll also get to hear information that no-one else has in their business area, adding considerable value to the role.

Barriers to good communication

Virtual working

We're all familiar with the challenges of working with a virtual team. Humans are designed to interact face to face, and we use all our senses – sight, sound, touch – to help us understand the message the other person is sending. When we can't use all of these senses, we look for clues among the information we do have. That's why small things like late responses, short emails and dead air on a conference call can cause so much stress.

There are several simple things you can do to combat this, outlined so

COMMUNICATING EFFECTIVELY

elegantly in the *Harvard Business Review*[13] that I'm going to quote from
it directly:

- **"Fight the 'illusion of transparency'.** We often think that others
  are more in synch with what we're thinking than they really are.
  The obvious fix for this illusion is greater empathy. Put yourself in
  the position of the other person. Actually visualize that individual
  in his office as you send him an email.

- **Amplify the signal.** We often communicate less information than
  we think we are, a syndrome psychologists call signal amplification
  bias. Don't just say, 'Circle back with me.' Do you want final input
  to a decision or just want to be informed of the decision after it's
  been made?

- **Respond promptly (if only to say you'll respond later).** In general,
  people will interpret the promptness of your response to an
  email or voice message as an indication of the quality of your
  relationship.

- **Encourage everyone to expect problems.** At the start of any virtual
  project, experts recommend a 'meta communication' of basic
  guidelines, such as how quickly people should respond to emails
  and what media should be used for which purposes (for instance,
  all team meetings will take place through videoconferencing).
  Setting the expectation that there will inevitably be problems
  makes everyone much less hesitant to raise an issue."

I'd add another piece of advice from my own experience: **ask direct
questions** about how things are going. Halfway through your call with a
champion, stop and ask 'Are you getting what you want from this call?'.

Since you're missing the physical cues, you need to replace them with directness and honesty.

Cultural differences

The advent of virtual working may mean that distance has lost much of its power, but geography and socio-economic differences have not.

Some cultures have very different views on what is considered appropriate communication – for example, punctuality, tone of voice and the etiquette of interruption. The most important tool you have to navigate this is to build a good relationship with each champion, and ask them directly how it is most appropriate to communicate with them. There are also plenty of websites where you can also research common pitfalls for different cultures.

Communicating with someone from a different culture is often as much about recovering from mistakes as it is about avoiding them. Accept that at some point you're bound to make a crashing error that requires an apology. You should do so swiftly and sincerely, and to the right people; bear in mind that your champion may need you to email or call a manager to ensure the apology is accepted. Then don't spend too much time beating yourself up about the mistake; you won't do it again!

Getting to know your champions

TUI Travel took an innovative route to addressing the differences between their champions. At one of their six-monthly champion conferences, they asked all champions to complete a personality

---

test – often used within the business to help teams understand each other's working style – and discussed the results in a session with an expert facilitator.

'It really helped us understand where everyone else was coming from,' says Kylie Bowen, network lead. 'When you saw people's names spread out across a model on the screen, you started to appreciate what mattered to them, and how we might tailor our communications for different champions. It also helped them to talk to each other more openly, in the session and beyond.'

One-to-many communications

One-to-many communications are what most network leads think of when the concept of 'communicating with your network' comes up – the schedule of conference calls and emails that keep momentum going within the group.

These communications are an efficient way of keeping champions up to date with the latest news, reminding them of the actions they're taking now, and chasing for reports. But you should also be aware of their limitations. Conference calls and emails do not allow for in-depth discussion or real honesty; if you need either of these, a one-to-one discussion is much better.

Video or conference calls

You should hold regular conference calls with champions, at least once a quarter, and more often in busy periods such as during sustainability reporting. I've chaired dozens of conference calls – some successful, some less so – and have developed my own set of rules for running them well.

- **Start with a clear purpose.** What's the call for? A general update where everyone will speak, a one-way communication where you present a new policy, or discussion of a specific topic? Everyone needs to be clear on this before the call starts, and have had time to read the relevant documents. (But never assume that everyone has read the pre-reads, so remember to review key points in the call.)

- **Enforce the ground rules.** As chair of the call, you are steward of everyone else's time. Always start promptly, even if some participants are late. If you need to, you should feel empowered to (respectfully) interrupt a champion mid-flow to keep the agenda on track.

- **Plan lots of one-to-one contact.** Participants usually stray off topic in a conference call because they see this as their best opportunity to be heard. The solution is almost always more one-to-one communication between you and the champion.

Matching the channel to the audience

TUI UK & Ireland's Retail Sustainability Champions rely on conference calls to communicate, as they meet very rarely. With 30 champions per call, it's certainly not something I would have recommended. . . but there are always exceptions!

'It works well for us,' says Rosie Bristow, the sustainability professional who supports the network lead, 'because Retail teams are used to huge conference calls; that's just part of the way they work. It's another of the ways in which having this network managed by a retail specialist has proven to be the right way forward: she knows that the champions will respond perfectly well to a call like this.

'We've also focused on platforms they know for their online communication. Retail teams already use Facebook for work purposes, so the champions themselves are planning to create a closed group. Their familiarity with Facebook should mean it's well used.'

Group emails

When we're asked to communicate with colleagues, most of us automatically start writing an email. But there are some clear drawbacks that mean you should think carefully before doing so. Emails don't always promote discussion, so they can rarely replace a real, live conversation.

If you are sending critical information via email, you should observe the following rules:

- **Keep the email as short as possible.** I've worked in plenty of networks where emails from the lead were regularly three pages or longer – and champions hardly ever read them. Keep emails to a maximum of six lines if you can; if it needs to be longer than that, give serious thought to a different medium.

- **Use the 'inverted pyramid' structure.** All budding journalists are taught to structure their stories in terms of the inverted pyramid: give a summary of all the relevant information in the first sentence, and then go into detail in the rest of the email. If your email contains a critical question for which you need a response, consider asking it upfront, in the first sentence, in bold type.

- **Copy in the right people.** The cc list of an email is often as important as what the email says. Copying someone's manager, for example, might be a courtesy, or it might indicate that you don't trust your champion to deliver. The best way to determine who should be copied into your network emails is simply to ask, and then respect your champion's wishes.

We get so many emails that it's hard to keep on top of them all. You can significantly increase the chances that your emails will be read by having a good track record of sending very few, and very clear, emails. You shouldn't be group emailing champions more than twice a week; once a week is even better.

One-to-one communications

Regular calls or meetings

The best way of building and maintaining trust with your champions is to speak to them regularly. The frequency of your calls is up to you, and it will take some experimentation to get the right balance.

If your sustainability network is into double figures, then completing a series of one-to-one calls can seem like a daunting task. It's tempting rely on group calls and emails to share information. Please try to resist this; there are real benefits to be gained from speaking to each champion individually.

- **Building your relationship.** If you don't speak one-to-one, you'll miss out on conversations that help you build trust and share (relevant) personal information. If a usually reliable champion hasn't submitted a report to you, doesn't it help to know that they have a significant deadline on another project?

- **Checking understanding and getting feedback.** Most champions won't admit in a group call that they don't understand what's being discussed. To make sure they have everything they need to carry out your actions, you need to speak to them directly and encourage them to be honest.

- **Live problem-solving.** You can often help solve problems by just talking them through with the champions. Many of us are able to work out how to solve problems (or at least how to take the next steps) when they're shared with an empathetic colleague.

Emails

Make sure you're the gatekeeper for all champion emails, and that your team understands that you will answer personally unless you explicitly agree otherwise. It sounds simple, but it can be a real time-waster if you're not clear about this from the start. One of the champions in a network I led once received separate responses from me, my manager, and her manager. . . which was not only confusing for them, but also rather embarrassing for us!

Always suggest a phone call if the question is complicated – it will save you time in the long run.

Reporting

The surest way of souring your relationship with your champions is ask them to measure and report on their work in a way that's onerous, repetitive, or that simply doesn't work. As the adage goes, you don't fatten a pig by weighing it.

Keep your champions' reporting burden as light as possible, and make sure you agree upfront what the processes are, why they're important, and when they should be completed.

- **Scorecard.** One of the champion's responsibilities will be to define annual targets for their business area, aligned with the global key performance indicators. The best way to see at a glance how each area is doing – and whether this adds up to real progress overall – is to provide a simple scorecard for champions. You should be clear about how often you expect to see an updated scorecard, and use it effectively: if there are areas that are falling short of expected progress, always follow up to find out if further support is needed.

- **Regular reports.** A scorecard is all very well, but it often doesn't capture a real flavour of what's happening. You might also ask for a regular report on progress that covers more qualitative issues such as the latest board reaction to sustainability, case studies and stories (useful to you for your own communications, both internal and external), and any problems they're encountering in delivering their workplan.

- **Annual sustainability reporting.** Once a year, you'll need detailed information from each of your champions for the sustainability report – and you may also need to ask some of them to be interviewed for an audit. Sustainability reports are often written by external companies who carry out interviews with champions, asking them the same questions they've just answered in their latest report to the network lead. You'll need a clear plan for ensuring they only provide information once.

Face-to-face meetings

It's important to have a physical one-to-one meeting with each of your champions at least once a year if you possibly can. For most network leads, the best opportunity will be around your champion conference (see below) when you can fit in meetings with all your champions.

In chapter 6, we discussed the importance of the contracting phase, where you allow each champion to be honest about their doubts and reservations. It's important to renew that contract regularly, review how the last year has gone and give them an opportunity to feed back on how they are feeling about their role.

Many-to-many communications

Ideally, your champions should support one another, as well as being supported by the network lead (see page 85 for more ideas on how to foster this support). Some of the best opportunities to encourage champions to support one another are through 'many-to-many' communications.

Online spaces

Online spaces can be invaluable for allowing champions to meet, talk and refer to key documents. But they need careful and appropriate management. The more features a collaborative website has, the more work it will take for you to manage it, so you should think carefully about what you want it to deliver. At the very minimum, I recommend you have somewhere to store your key documents – for example, standard presentations on sustainability, guidelines for reporting, key policies and other documents.

Champions may want a channel of communication with their peers without the urgency of email, and online spaces can be a great way of fostering collaboration between disparate parts of the network. You can do this with a very light touch, using a platform that your champions already know (such as Facebook), and leaving them to contact one another as they wish.

Champion conferences

I recommend you hold a champion conference – an opportunity for your network to meet, discuss key topics and get the latest updated – at least once a year. You can vary the location of the conference so that different champions can host; it's a great opportunity for them to show off a local project and for you to meet the senior management of their business area.

The conference can be a collaborative event if you allow it to, by letting interested champions chair different sessions, and bring their own views to the table. You could even put aside a whole session for champions to share their experience, letting champions with a difficult challenge host tables of their peers, so that they can share their own solutions.

Don't forget that a conference is an opportunity to develop deeper links between your champions and to revisit your goals and how they feel about them. Try not to add too many 'business as usual' items to the agenda.

Using conferences creatively

As you would expect from a travel and tourism company, TUI Travel's Global Sustainability Coordinators are used to travelling, and meet for a face-to-face conference twice a year.

Each champion takes a turn to host the two-day conference in their offices, and many of them have used this opportunity to do something a little bit more creative.

'When we held our champion conference in Stockholm, the host champion asked for an hour slot for lunch on the second day, and wouldn't tell us why,' says Kylie Bowen, network lead. 'When lunchtime rolled around, two cabin crew suddenly appeared with an airline lunch and started serving it to all the attendees.

'One of our airlines, TUIfly Nordic, had recently developed a smartphone app to help cabin crew measure waste and recycling on board, and we were treated to a live demonstration. As sustainability champions, of course we tried to recycle as much of the material as humanly possible! It was a great way to introduce their new initiative, and it certainly sparked off lots of creativity in the other champions.'

CHAPTER 8

Getting the Best Out of Your Network

ONCE YOUR NETWORK IS UP AND RUNNING, you'll need to make decisions everyday on how often to contact them, what to ask of them, and when to intervene in their work, keeping a constant eye on the balance between pushing the champions and standing back.

Throughout my years as a network lead, I've made these decisions in all sorts of ways. Sometimes the decisions have been good, and sometime my solutions have fallen flat. This section covers the lessons I've learned, in no particular order. . .

Make sure your role adds value

Your role as network lead needs to add clear value to champions. If they don't see why they need you – and it's a common perception of global roles that they exist only to create more work for the people who deliver – you won't get the buy-in you need to transform the company.

The value you add is likely to fall into one of the categories below:

- Access to senior management

- Increased profile for the champion

- Networking opportunities – particularly with international businesses

- Coaching, training and knowledge

- Better understanding of how the targets can be met

There will be other ways in which you add value in your particular context. It's worth taking some time to write down what you do, and create an 'elevator pitch' for your role, because you are likely to find you need to justify it frequently, both to your champions and to those who hold the sustainability purse-strings.

Make your champions feel valued

The evidence tells us that the key to motivating people is to make them feel valued. In my experience, it doesn't take much effort to do this well: noticing good work, responding promptly to requests for help, and sending useful snippets of information every now and again all take a relatively short amount of time.

It's those small acts of feedback that are easy to dismiss as surplus to requirements, but each small contact demonstrates that you've thought of them, and understood them well enough to send them something truly relevant. That's an important part of building a relationship.

Formalise their role

It should go without saying, but if your champion's sustainability responsibilities aren't part of their personal objectives, all the motivation in the world won't help them find the time to complete them. Personal objectives are the business of the employee and their line manager, so you need to tread carefully – but for part-time champions you should expect to see the relevant objective(s) in order to ensure they are specific, measurable, and in line with the global sustainability goals.

Don't overload them

It's easy to look at the year stretching out ahead and to fill it with activities: reporting takes up several months, then there's a champion conference, a new policy to write and sign off, an employee engagement campaign, case study gathering for the company conference, and a change to the scorecard methodology. Before you know it, you're back in reporting season.

Don't forget: your champions' first priority is to deliver their local sustainability plan, so don't overload them with work on behalf of the global team. If they are part-time champions, they'll also have another role to deliver as well!

You can help them in several ways:

- **Set a clear schedule.** Include the estimated time needed to complete each champion task. It's important to understand your champions' other commitments, and when they are likely to be most busy. Always involve them in setting the schedule, to avoid any clashes.

- **Prioritise.** The best way to do this is to ask for two levels of action on each task: the compulsory, simple level and the optional, stretching level. Those champions who have the capacity and the buy-in can complete the stretching level.

- **Offer practical opportunities for action.** Most sustainability networks run at least one high-profile global event each year that champions can roll out locally. You can provide template materials for champions to localise, run an employee competition for them to advertise, and centralise the activity around a specific date.

- **Use working groups for specific topics.** If you're reviewing a global policy, for example, or planning a report, set up a separate working group of interested champions. That way, champions who do not have the capacity to contribute can opt out of the conversation.

- **Allow them regular breaks.** Some of the most successful projects are managed with participants' energy in mind. Tony Schwartz recommends you should schedule work in three-week sprints, allowing team members time to relax and renew in between.[14] For champions, you might want to schedule in three-week projects designed to fit alongside their other commitments.

Push the leaders

If they can't see the added value for their point in the sustainability journey, leading countries, departments or brands can start to feel disillusioned with the network. There are a few ways to combat this:

- **Help them access the support they need.** For example, would it benefit them to meet sustainability managers from other companies that have taken a step beyond theirs? Can they attend external conferences to help them stretch their thinking?

- **Highlight what they can learn from other champions.** Everyone has areas of sustainability in which they could improve. You can 'buddy' them with a champion from another area of the business if you think they have things to teach each other.

- **Formalise their mentoring relationships.** Leaders are often engaged in unofficial mentoring of other champions. Formalising this can add real value for them, especially if you offer training to help their career progression. You might even consider seconding them into the global team for a few months so that they can see how key decisions are made.

Support the laggards

It's not a lot of fun to be lagging behind your peers. Champions from less advanced business areas are likely to feel despondent and powerless, even if it's not their fault. You can help them by doing the following:

- **Set clear priorities for them.** It's easy to feel paralysed when you see how much work there is to be done to reach the same level as the leaders. As the network lead, you can help them understand the most important actions to take now, and which can wait. For champions at the very beginning of embedding sustainability, goals based on building relationships may be more appropriate than hard targets.

- **Offer practical support.** Many of the barriers at the initial stages of a sustainability plan are to do with a lack of management buy-in, and you can help with this. Offer them access to senior members of the global team to help them convince their board that sustainability matters to the business.

- **Help with quick wins for their area.** New champions often find themselves in a Catch-22 situation: they don't have the resource they need to achieve their sustainability goals, but can't secure that resource before they've proved they can deliver results. You can help them identify the projects they can take on and deliver quickly, so that they can ask for additional resource.

Intervene quickly where you need to

Once you know your champions well, you'll be able to spot immediately when something is not as it should be. Sometimes champions ask for help directly; but often it's a change in behaviour – for example, silence where there's usually chatter – that will let you know there's a problem.

However you find out, it's important to air the issue as soon as possible. Encourage them to tell you about it by practicing 'active listening' – reflecting back what they're saying and summarising regularly to show you've heard them – rather than trying to solve the problem yourself.

Then you can work with them to decide on next steps. Together, list all the things you might do to solve the problem. There might be an obvious solution or you might need to obtain guidance from someone else; but make sure you don't leave the phone call until you've agreed a plan of action.

Focus on the positives

As well as keeping an eye out for problems, make sure you keep looking for the 'bright spots' (see page 64). We tend to spend more energy fixing things that are going wrong rather than building on things that are working. It's just as important to celebrate and spread best practice, so that champions stay motivated and have a clear idea of the results they're aiming for.

In the worst cases, great results invite suspicion rather than celebration, or can be presented in a way that gives others permission to aim lower. For a long time, I talked of the outstanding results of one of my champions this way: 'Brazil has done X, Y and Z, which is brilliant. But, of course, sustainability is better understood there.' I thought I was helping contextualise the results and making the less successful champions feel better – but I soon stopped when I realised that I wasn't helping. In fact, I was sabotaging their efforts by defining the Brazilian results as 'out of their reach'.

Encourage champions to support each other

The ultimate goal of having a network is for the champions to build relationships with *each other* as well as with you. That's not only because it will reduce the burden on you as network lead – though that's a laudable goal in itself – but also because, in many cases, help from a fellow champion will be more effective than from the network lead.

As Chip and Dan Heath outline in *Making It Stick*,[15] even if you know the solution to a particular issue – let's call it Problem X – you may not be able to offer it to the right champions because Problem X doesn't always look the same. For example, you may see a lack of progress on a particular goal, and think your champion hasn't made enough effort. But another champion might identify a different problem: the measurement of this goal has not been well defined, so their progress is not being captured.

Groups of people don't just automatically start thinking of themselves as a network, sharing stories and offering support, and it takes time and hard work to create the right conditions for this to happen. Here are some ideas to get you started:

- **Encourage champions to talk when you're not present.** Circulate lists of champions, create an online space where they

GETTING THE BEST
OUT OF YOUR NETWORK

introduce themselves and can chat using forums or messengers
– anything you can think of as long as it's run by champions, for
champions.

• **Help champions widen their own networks.** Run 'speed dating'
sessions at conferences where they get to meet everyone else,
pair them up with champions they don't know during breakout
sessions, and put them in touch to discuss specific issues where
you think they have something in common.

• **Buddy them up with other champions.** Mentoring relationships
can be as formal or informal as you like, and buddying is well
known as way to getting new champions up to speed. But even
experienced champions can gain value from being partnered with
someone in a similar role.

Experiencing sustainability together

Soon after they were formed and trained, TUI UK's Retail
sustainability champions went on a trip to Turkey to see first-hand
some of the projects that the company is supporting there.

'That's where they really started to become a network,' says Rosie
Bristow, Sustainability Communications and Planning Manager.
'They saw sustainability in action and came back committed to
making a difference – but they also spent time with each other
and started to make the individual links that are vital for them to
work together as a network.'

Ask for feedback

We're all learning how to embed sustainability into our companies – how to set stretching goals, how best to deliver them, and how to work well with one another. That means it pays to ask for feedback from your network regularly.

Give your champions specific opportunities to feed back: for example, after a meeting, call or conference, or when the sustainability report has been put to bed. Ask questions in a way that elicits honest feedback rather than encourages champions to tell you everything was fine. My favourite is 'What's the one thing we could have done better?'

Don't forget to heed Ernest Hemingway, who said, 'When people talk, listen completely. Most people never listen.' That means you should not only solicit feedback, but you need to make it clear you have acted on it. Showing champions that you take their views seriously will encourage them to speak up next time.

CHAPTER 9

Embrace Difficulties

MILITARY LEADERS HAVE UNDERSTOOD for millennia that no plan survives contact with the enemy. No matter how robust your sustainability strategy when it's written, you'll almost certainly find that you need to change some of your plans once you actually get going.

As internal consultants, we should expect what *Flawless Consulting*[16] refers to as 'resistance' from our clients. What's more, we should learn to love it, because it's an integral part of the process of change.

Change your view of resistance

Resistance is an inevitable – and, indeed, necessary – part of the consultant–client relationship. If your sustainability goals are sufficiently stretching, you should be able to see where you want to get to and plan the first few steps, but the middle of your journey will remain unclear. That should be scary and uncomfortable for all concerned.

If you don't experience some level of resistance from our champions, it's a signal that they're not committed to creating real change, or that your sustainability goals aren't stretching enough. So the real test of your network, and of you as network lead, isn't how smoothly the relationships go at all times – rather, it's how you respond to problems arising. (It's worth making sure that your manager, or whoever judges your success, knows this, or you could be heading for a bad review!)

Spotting resistance

Organisations are political places, and managers value power and control. The loss of either of these causes anxiety – in fact, humans react to a threat to their social standing in the same way as to a threat to their physical survival.[17]

Most people don't feel comfortable expressing themselves directly at work. In our modern business culture, which emphasises problem-solving, sociability and the 'can-do' attitude, it's tough to be honest about your anxieties: that you're losing control, don't have the right skills, don't feel equipped to deliver your goals, have too much on, or are worried that your manager doesn't support you.

So, if they're feeling anxious, your champions are likely to express their anxieties in more subtle ways. You may find them repeating sentences such as the following: 'You have to understand that. . .', 'Let me explain something to you' or 'I want to make sure this is not an academic exercise.'

Notice how each of these is a legitimate expression of a problem – but it's your problem, not theirs. It may be, of course, that the problem does really lie with you. But if you can answer honestly that you believe there's no real reason for them to push back on your suggestions, it's probably a sign of resistance.

Dealing with resistance

The basic strategy for managing resistance is not to fight it. Champions feel the way they feel, and there's no sense in arguing that they should feel differently. The best way through the storm is to help the champion express their feelings directly. You need to deal with, not overcome, resistance.

Peter Brock identifies three steps for handling resistance:

1. '**Identify in your own mind what form the resistance is taking.** The skill is to pick up the cues from the manager and then describe to yourself what you see happening.

2. **State, in a neutral, unpunishing way, the form the resistance is taking.** This is called "naming the resistance." The skill is to find the neutral language.

3. **Be quiet.** Let the line manager respond to your statement about the resistance.'

In my experience, it's the third step that is often the hardest to do. It feels strange in a business context to make a statement about feelings and then to stop talking. But with some practice, it's the most effective way to communicate authentically with your champions.

How to deal with specific problems

Below, I've identified some forms of resistance that I experienced as a network lead. You may want to take a moment to write down some of your own, so that you're prepared for the next time you experience this form of resistance.

What they say	What it means	What to do
'I need more information before I can start'	Sometimes this reaction is justified – your champion really doesn't have the information they need – but it's often a hidden form of resistance. The inkling that there's a problem should come if you're answering question after question clearly and in full, but you're beginning to get irritated by the never-ending stream of additional questions.	Try asking: 'You seem unsure about what we are discussing. Is this because we're not defining the problem well, or are you not sure what to do about it?'
'You don't understand: my business area is different'	This is another reasonable objection to the work you're doing with a champion – but you need to know when to stop tailoring your strategy to the needs of their business area, and start recognising resistance.	Try the following: 'We've done a lot of work on this programme, but we don't seem to be getting closer to something that works. How are you feeling about this?'
'This just won't work in the real world'	Again, this might be true. . . but if your other champions are making it work, this is likely to be resistance rather than a real objection.	See above.

What they say	What it means	What to do
'Yes, of course'	Some champions are happy to agree to everything you ask of them – but when it comes to the crunch, they don't deliver. They may be finding it difficult for them to let you know that they don't have the skills, capacity or support to deliver what you're asking. This is more common in some cultures than others, especially if it's not the done thing to refuse a request from a manager.	This might work: 'You seem willing to do anything I suggest. I'm happy for you to tell me if there's too much to deliver in this programme, and we work together to prioritise the actions. I can't tell how you really feel about this.'

What they say	What it means	What to do
(Silence)	When a champion doesn't report back to you properly, there could be several reasons: busy schedules, unsupportive managers, or confusing instructions. But one of the possible explanations is that they don't see the value of the network, and want to limit the time they spend on your work.	Show them the value you add, and fill in the big picture for them: why you need cooperation from them, and what you're all working for together. It often helps to meet face to face, and encourage them to be honest. Depending on how they react, you can ask, 'You are really questioning a lot of what I do. You seem angry about something' or 'You are very quiet. I don't know how to read your silence.'

What they say	What it means	What to do
'Oooops'	This one's not really an example of resistance, but I've included it because it's one of the most common practical problems you're likely to encounter. Both of these things have happened to me: finding out (often from a third party) that a local sustainability report I hadn't heard of has been launched – or, worse, that a local advertising campaign I didn't know about has been accused of greenwash.	Try to be as honest with your champion as possible. For example, you might say, 'It makes me uncomfortable to hear this through a third party. It makes me feel vulnerable because I don't have information I'm expected to have.' Hopefully, you'll be able to agree a plan of action to put things right without causing a permanent rupture in your relationship.

Letting go

Sometimes, naming the resistance and encouraging honesty won't work. There might be a real barrier behind the champion's resistance that you didn't see, or the champion simply may not want to carry out the action, no matter how much you help them.

In these situations, you need to be prepared to let go and accept there's nothing you can do about it right now. The level of 'letting go' will vary depending on the situation.

- If you're experiencing strong resistance on a specific part of your strategy you should let it go, at least temporarily. Come back to it next year, or when the champion is less busy, or when you see them face to face. Not everything can be achieved right now.

- If you're getting very little cooperation from your champion but their results are good, don't invest too much time in them. You may have a better relationship with them later on: perhaps a new manager will impress upon them the importance of working with you, or something else will shift in the company that means they become more interested. Or they may even be replaced with someone more enthusiastic.

- If your champion is showing lots of resistance and not delivering, you may need to find a new champion. Make sure you ask the champion directly if they would rather not continue, and hold conversations with your manager and theirs, preferably together. There need be no stigma in passing on the role to someone else if it's not right for this person.

You should always talk to your manager before you decide to do any of these things. They may be able to add insight into the problem, pull strings at senior levels, or speak to the champion's manager to find out what's going on. At the very least, you need to protect yourself from an accusation of not trying hard enough to deliver your strategy.

....

CHAPTER 10

Preparing for The Future

CONGRATULATIONS ON YOUR NEW (or revamped) network! Now you can relax and just watch the network tick over. . . right?

Sorry to disappoint, but that's not quite how it works. As the external environment changes, the risks and opportunities for your business will change as well. Businesses themselves are in a constant state of flux – quite apart from the managed change programmes they implement at regular intervals – and your network will need to change to keep ahead of the game.

Your sustainability strategy will grow and develop, hopefully getting closer and closer to core business strategy, and that will mean you and your champions will need to develop new strategies, new arguments and new skills to deliver targets and mobilise your colleagues.

The sustainability network is a long-term investment, and it's unlikely ever to reach a steady state if you're responding effectively to the company's needs.

So how do you keep up?

Make some friends

One of the best ways of keeping up to date with the latest sustainability challenges and finding out how other companies are responding is to get out of the office and meet other sustainability professionals. Most cities have a good calendar of conferences and networking events. If you're not keen on busy rooms, you'd be surprised how many managers are more than happy to chat over a cup of coffee.

The other benefit of talking to other people in the same position is that you'll soon find the terrible and unique challenges you face with your network are, in fact, pretty commonplace. The more you extend your own external network, the faster you'll pick up on trends and new ideas for your champions.

Look after yourself

It's a fundamental truth of life that there is always more to do than time to do it. Trying to get everything done at once is a recipe for disaster, and no matter how much you managed to achieve before you finally succumbed to the inevitable, a burned-out network lead can't add any value at all.

Working in sustainability is a particularly stressful place to be (or does everyone think that about their role?) because it's your job to be one step ahead of your organisation. It can sometimes feel as if everyone hates you: your colleagues for moving too fast, and external stakeholders for not moving fast enough.

You need to make sure you 'fill your own bucket' by taking on only the work you can cope with, making sure you get enough rest, and looking after yourself, physically and mentally. Taking time out for yourself can seem indulgent when you're working for 'the cause' – but you'll soon find that doing so allows you to be a much better network lead for your champions.

TUI Travel: ahead of the game

TUI Travel's Group Sustainability Coordinators, spread across key markets and departments, have been working as a network for several years now, in a company where other Group functions have historically operated with a lighter touch.

'Recently, the Group decided to work more closely on key strategic issues,' says Kylie Bowen, network lead, 'And it's meant that we became a source of advice on how to run a Groupwide network, and seen as real pioneers across the business. We weren't expecting that!'

Be prepared to change everything

When you first start to change something, inertia – the tendency of objects to keep moving in the same direction at the same speed – is working against you. It can be hard work to keep going in the face of resistance. But you should also to be prepared for the day when your hard work begins to pay off and inertia starts to work in your favour.

How will you cope when sustainability activities proliferate faster than you can keep up with them? Will your network still be a valuable resource, or a relic of a time when 'champions' and 'non-champions' were viable categories?

Toby Radcliffe, network lead at EDF Energy, described his goal for the Company Makers in this way: 'We're starting with tiny pinpricks of light – the champions – and we want this to grow first into a web of light, and then into a glow everywhere.'

It makes sense to be on the lookout for the 'weak signals' that give you clues about how the company – and the world – will look in a few years' time. One of the main topics of conversation in 2013 has been the sustainability strategy versus the business strategy informed by sustainability. What does that mean for your network? Will you move from delivering on targets to fostering a sustainable way of doing business? Who will you need to bring into your network to help with this?

Don't worry about this too much right now. It will be a long time until your network becomes obsolete; the leading companies in sustainability have more, not fewer, networks than everyone else, because they recognise the scale of the challenge. At the beginning of the journey, it's hard to imagine what the middle will look like, because so many things will have changed by the time you get there.

In the meantime, keep in mind the words of the psychologist William James: 'Act as if what you do makes a difference. It does.'

Notes

1. Doughty Centre, Cranfield School of Management, 2009. *Corporate Responsibility Champions Network: A 'How to' Guide*, February.

2. Doughty Centre, Cranfield School of Management, February 2009. *Corporate Responsibility Champions Network: A 'How to' Guide*, February.

3. Cantor, David E., Morrow, Paula C. and Montabon, Frank, 2012. Engagement in environmental behaviors among supply chain management employees: An organizational support theoretical perspective. *Journal of Supply Chain Management* (Volume 48 Issue 3): 33–51.

4. Ordonez, Lisa D., Schweitzer, Maurice E., Galinsky, Adam D. and Braverman, Max H., 2009. Goals gone wild: The systematic side-effects of over-prescribing goal setting. Harvard Business School Working Paper No. 09-083, February.

5. Brock, Peter, 1999. *Flawless Consulting: A Guide to Getting Your Expertise Used*

6. Brock, Peter, 1999. *Flawless Consulting: A Guide to Getting Your Expertise Used*

7. Doughty Centre, Cranfield School of Management, 2009. *Corporate Responsibility Champions Network: A 'How to' Guide*, February.

8. http://www.ted.com/talks/brene_brown_on_vulnerability.html

9. Doughty Centre, Cranfield School of Management, 2009. *Corporate Responsibility Champions Network: A 'How to' Guide*, February.

10. Molinsky, Andy and Zakkour, Michael, 2013. When best practices don't travel. HBR Blog Network, April, **http://blogs.hbr.org/2013/04/when-best-practices-dont-travel/**

NOTES

11. Heath, Chip and Heath, Dan, 2011. *Switch: How To Change Things When Change Is Hard*

12. Doughty Centre, Cranfield School of Management, 2009. *Corporate Responsibility Champions Network: A 'How to' Guide*, February.

13. Ferrazzi, Keith, 2013. How to avoid virtual miscommunication. HBR Blog Network, April, **http://blogs.hbr.org/2013/04/how-to-avoid-virtual-miscommun/**

14. Schwartz, Tony, with Gomes, Jean and McCarthy, Catherine, 2010. *The Way We're Working Isn't Working* (New York: Simon & Schuster).

15. Heath, Chip and Heath, Dan, 2008. *Made to Stick: Why Some Ideas Take Hold and Others Come Unstuck* (New York: Random House).

16. Brock, Peter, 1999. *Flawless Consulting: A Guide to Getting Your Expertise Used*

17. Dickerson, Sally S., Gruenewald, Tara L. and Kemeny, Margaret E., 2004. When the social self is threatened: shame, physiology, and health. *Journal of Personality* (Volume 72, Issue 6): 1191–1216.

For Product Safety Concerns and Information please contact our EU
representative GPSR@taylorandfrancis.com
Taylor & Francis Verlag GmbH, Kaufingerstraße 24, 80331 München, Germany